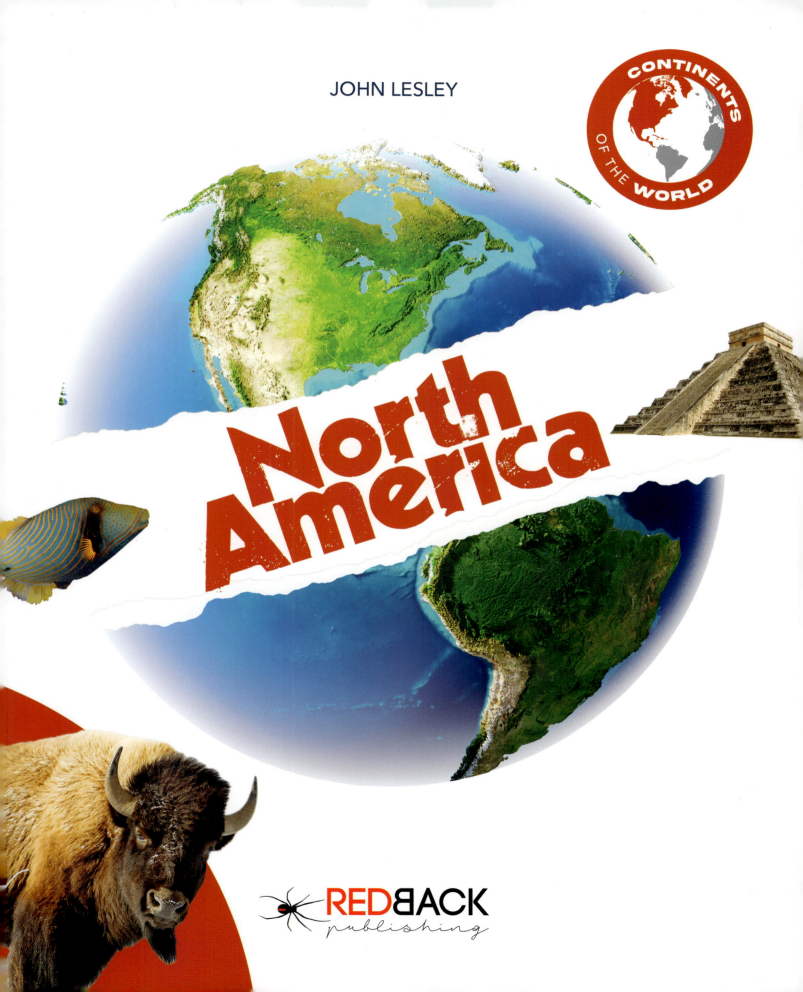

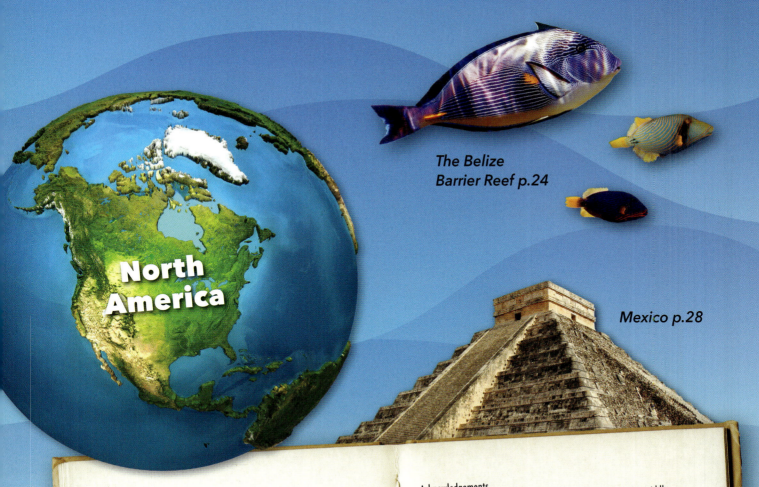

The Belize Barrier Reef p.24

Mexico p.28

North America

Redback Publishing
PO Box 357 Frenchs Forest NSW 2086
Australia

www.redbackpublishing.com.au
orders@redbackpublishing.com.au

© Redback Publishing 2023

ISBN 978-1-922322-50-0 HBK

All rights reserved.
No part of this publication may be reproduced in any form or by any means (including photocopying or storing it in any medium by electronic means and whether or not transiently or incidentally to some other use of this publication) without the written permission of the copyright owner. Applications for the copyright owner's written permission should be addressed to the publisher.

Author: John Lesley
Editor: Caroline Thomas
Designer: Redback Publishing

Original illustrations © Redback Publishing 2023

Originated by Redback Publishing

Acknowledgements
Abbreviations: l—left, r—right, b—bottom, t—top, c—centre, m—middle
We would like to thank the following for permission to reproduce photographs (images © Shutterstock unless otherwise stated):
p7tr Mexico City, Mexico, Joshua Davenport, p7mr New york City, USA, View Apart, p10bl washington, DC, USA, Paul Hakimata Photography, p10br Saint Kitts and Nevis, EQRoy, p20-21 Panama Canal, Solarisys, p26br Quebec, Canada, Wangkun Jia, p27tr Greenland, Brendan Delany, p27mr 1973 Greenland stamp, neftali, p27c Greenland glaciers, oliverdelahaye, p30tr Holy Week procession in Guatemala, Mokuba90

Disclaimer
Every effort has been made to contact copyright holders of any material reproduced in this book. Any omissions will be rectified in subsequent printings if notice is given to the publisher.

 A catalogue record for this book is available from the National Library of Australia

Contents

Earth's 7 Continents 4
Origin of North America 5
The Continent of North America 6
North America's Continental Shelf 8
The People of North America 10
Landscapes 12
Longest Rivers 12
Mountain Ranges 14
Volcanoes and Earthquakes 16
Special Places in North America 18
The Belize Barrier Reef 24
The Caribbean 24
Canada 26
Greenland 27
Mexico 28
United States 29
Religions 30
   Glossary 31
      Index 32

Greenland p.27

Special Places in North America p.18

The People of North America p.10

Earth's 7 Continents

What is a continent?
A continent is a very large landmass which is separated from others on Earth. Some are separated by oceans, but others have land borders with each other.

How many continents are there on Earth?
There are seven continents

1. Europe
2. Asia
3. Australia
4. Antarctica
5. Africa
6. South America
7. North America

Or are there 5?
Some people group Europe and Asia into one continent called Eurasia, and they combine North and South America into the Americas. According to this method of counting, there are five continents instead of seven.

Origin of North America

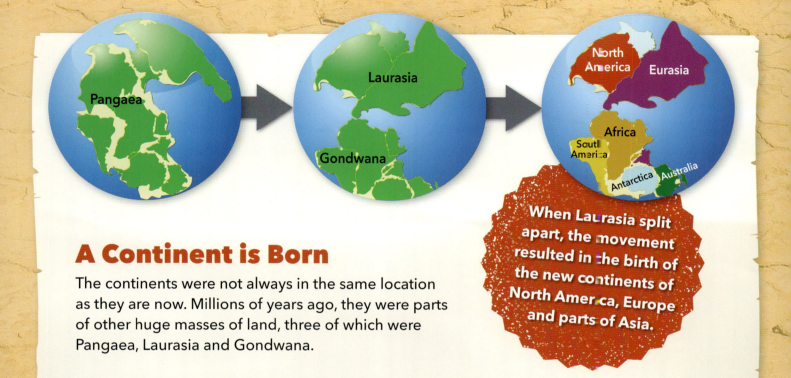

A Continent is Born

The continents were not always in the same location as they are now. Millions of years ago, they were parts of other huge masses of land, three of which were Pangaea, Laurasia and Gondwana.

When Laurasia split apart, the movement resulted in the birth of the new continents of North America, Europe and parts of Asia.

How did the continents form?

The rocky surface of our planet is constantly moving in a process called plate tectonics. As massive blocks of rock separate, they move across the surface of Earth, forming the continents we know today.

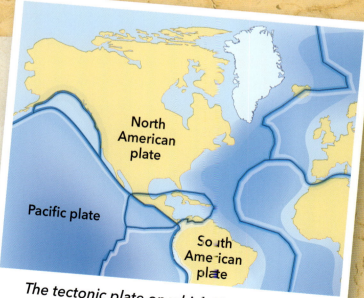

The tectonic plate on which North America sits is still moving, but at the very slow rate of a few centimetres each year.

The Continent of North America

UNITED STATES

Climate of North America

The North American climates range from tropical to temperate, and arid to arctic.

Parts of Canada and Greenland are only a few hundred kilometres from the North Pole. Panama at the far south of North America has a hot, tropical climate.

North America's Continental Shelf

Prehsitoric animals such as the woolly mammoth roamed through North America during the last Ice Age.

Where a continent meets the ocean, the land at the edge often continues under the water as a continental shelf. This shelf may stop abruptly at a point where the underwater rocks drop down to a deep ocean abyss.

During the last Ice Age, which ended about 10,000 years ago, some of these continental shelves were dry land, making the continents much bigger than they are today.

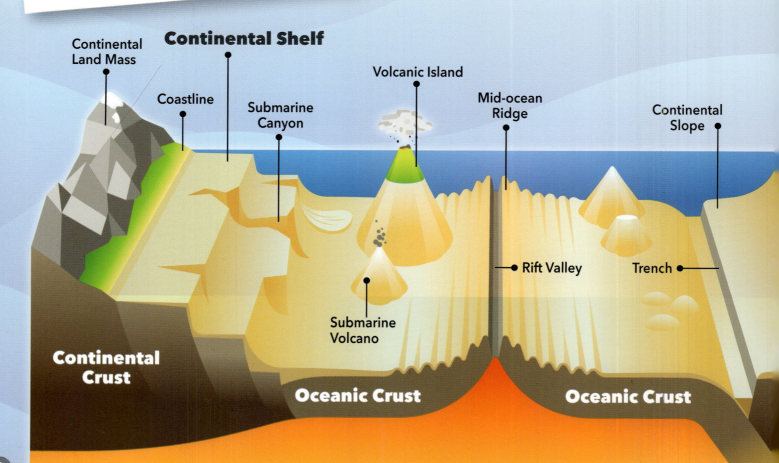

Where are North America's borders?

None of the Earth's seven continents have a definite border. Nations define the exact borders of their country, but not of the continent on which that country lies.

At an ocean boundary, each country in North America can claim control over the ocean and the continental shelf for a distance of 200 nautical miles from the shore. Member countries of the United Nations set this distance under the UNCLOS agreement.

UNCLOS

The United Nations Convention on the Law of the Sea (UNCLOS) sets rules that countries use to determine who has control over the water and the seafloor at a nation's ocean boundary.

Arctic Ocean
Pacific Ocean
North America
Atlantic Ocean

North America's southern boundary is where it meets the continent of South America.

Continental Land Mass
Volcano
Continental Crust

RUSSIA — Bering Strait — ALASKA (UNITED STATES)

Some scientists believe that the continental shelf that is now under the Bering Strait, between Alaska and Russia, was dry land thousands of years ago. This may have been one of the routes taken when people from Asia walked into the North American continent for the first time. Even today, the strait is just over 80 kilometres wide at its narrowest point.

9

The People of North America

How Many People?

Nearly 600 million people live across the whole North American continent.

The United States has the largest population on the continent, with about 330 million people.

The smallest nation in the North American continent is Saint Kitts and Nevis, an island in the Caribbean. Its population is only about 50,000 people.

United States of America: about 330 million people

Saint Kitts and Nevis: about 50,000 people

The First People

The ancestors of the indigenous people of North America possibly arrived there 40,000 years ago. At this time in Earth's history there was an Ice Age which lowered sea levels. This could have allowed people to migrate from northern Asia into North America.

Living in the Frozen North

The indigenous peoples themselves have their own histories which place their ancestors in North America from the very beginning of their existence on Earth.

The Inuit, who were once called Eskimos, developed ways to live in the frozen north. They invented igloos and hunted a variety of animals that provided them with food, fur and hides.

Christopher Columbus

Christopher Columbus arrived in Central America in 1492. He took word back to Spain that the Americas existed. This news encouraged the European colonisation of the Americas.

Landscapes

North America is so large that it has a wide variety of landscapes.

Treeless Arctic tundra

Pine forests

Grassy plains

Longest Rivers

Mississippi River

Rio Grande

Missouri River

Mountain Ranges

The two largest mountain ranges in North America are the Appalachian Mountains and the Rocky Mountains.

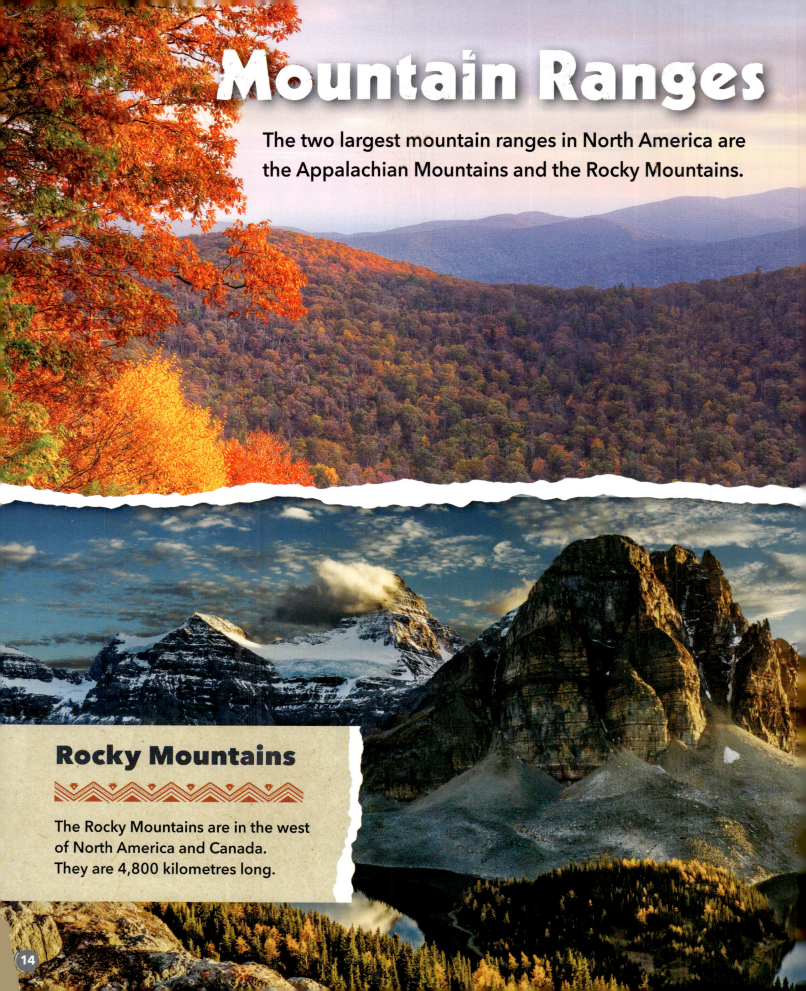

Rocky Mountains

The Rocky Mountains are in the west of North America and Canada. They are 4,800 kilometres long.

Appalachian Mountains

The Appalachian Mountains in the east of the United States and Canada extend for 3,200 kilometres. They are densely wooded and posed a barrier to early European explorers who could not find an easy way to cross them. Once they did, settlers followed, and the interior became colonised.

Volcanoes and Earthquakes

San Andreas Fault

In North America there are two tectonic plates of the Earth's crust that are sliding past each other. As they move, they cause earthquakes. The famous San Francisco earthquake of 1906, when large parts of the city were destroyed, was a result of this sort of movement. The fire that followed the earthquake added another disaster for the residents to endure.

A number of cities are located right on or near the San Andreas Fault. These include Los Angeles and San Francisco. Hollywood, famous for its movie industry, is also near this fault line.

Scientists believe that another big earthquake could occur in this region at any time.

Canada

Many earthquakes occur along the west coast of Canada. This is a result of complex tectonic plate activity in that region.

Although Canada's west coast is on the infamous Pacific Ring of Fire, where there are many volcanoes, there has not been an eruption in Canada for over 200 years.

Yellowstone National Park

Located in the United States, Yellowstone National Park is a large area of hot springs, geysers and bubbling mud. All this thermal activity comes from a hot spot in the Earth's crust below Yellowstone.

A large part of Yellowstone consists of the remains of a gigantic volcanic eruption that happened about 600,000 years ago.

Yellowstone has a herd of rare bison, an animal that was once almost extinct.

Mount St Helens

Mount St Helens is an active volcano in the US state of Washington. It erupted destructively in 1980. Deep under the surface, two tectonic plates are moving against each other, producing the heat that led to the volcano erupting at the surface.

The tsunami's height by comparison

Burj Khalifa

Empire State Building

Eiffel Tower

Tsunami in Alaska

In 1958, a **tsunami** caused by an earthquake in Lituya Bay, Alaska, reached heights of over 500 metres as it flooded across the shore and onto land.

Lituya Bay

Special Places in North America

❶ Grand Canyon

The Grand Canyon is a deep gorge, carved by the Colorado River in the United States. At some points it is over 1,800 metres deep.

❷ Great Lakes

Lake Superior is the largest lake in North America. It is one of the five Great Lakes that are on and near the border between Canada and the United States. The lakes contain 20% of all the fresh water that is on the surface of the Earth.

Such a large body of inland fresh water helps to make the surrounding climate moderate. This is an advantage for local agriculture.

❸ Panama Canal

Ships travelling from the Atlantic to the Pacific Ocean coasts of North America once had to sail all the way south to the Strait of Magellan in South America to get from one side of the continent to the other. This changed when the Panama Canal opened in 1914.

This manmade canal allows a ship to pass along a waterway that is very narrow in some places. It reaches the other side of the continent in only 65 kilometres instead of thousands.

❹ Northwest Passage

Another sea route between the east and west of North America is the Northwest Passage. This route takes ships through Arctic waters.

⑤ Niagara Falls

The Niagara Falls are located on the border between Canada and the United States. The largest of the three waterfalls is Horseshoe Falls, which drops over 50 metres. The force of the flow of water over the edge is slowly wearing away the rocky ledge.

6 The Great Plains

The Great Plains are in the central parts of the United States and stretch north into Canada as prairies. The farmland of the Great Plains produces an enormous amount of agricultural produce, especially wheat, corn and beef.

Before colonisation, the Great Plains were the home of many indigenous peoples, including the Blackfoot, Cheyenne and Comanche.

Corn Crops

The indigenous people of Central America were the first to grow crops of maize (corn), now one of the world's most important foods.

Today, corn is the main crop grown in the United States, much of it in the Great Plains. Corn is eaten by people and farm animals, and it can be used to make ethanol for car fuel.

Without corn we would not have popcorn!

The Belize Barrier Reef

The World's Second Largest Coral Reef

The world's second largest coral reef grows on the continental shelf off Belize in Central America. (The Great Barrier Reef in Australia is the longest coral reef anywhere.)

The Carribean

Sweet Sugar

Sugarcane is an important crop in some of the Caribbean nations, where it has been grown in plantations since the 1600s.

Tourism Trail
Tourism is a major industry across the whole Caribbean region.

Many of the Caribbean islands are of coral reef or volcanic origins.

Canada

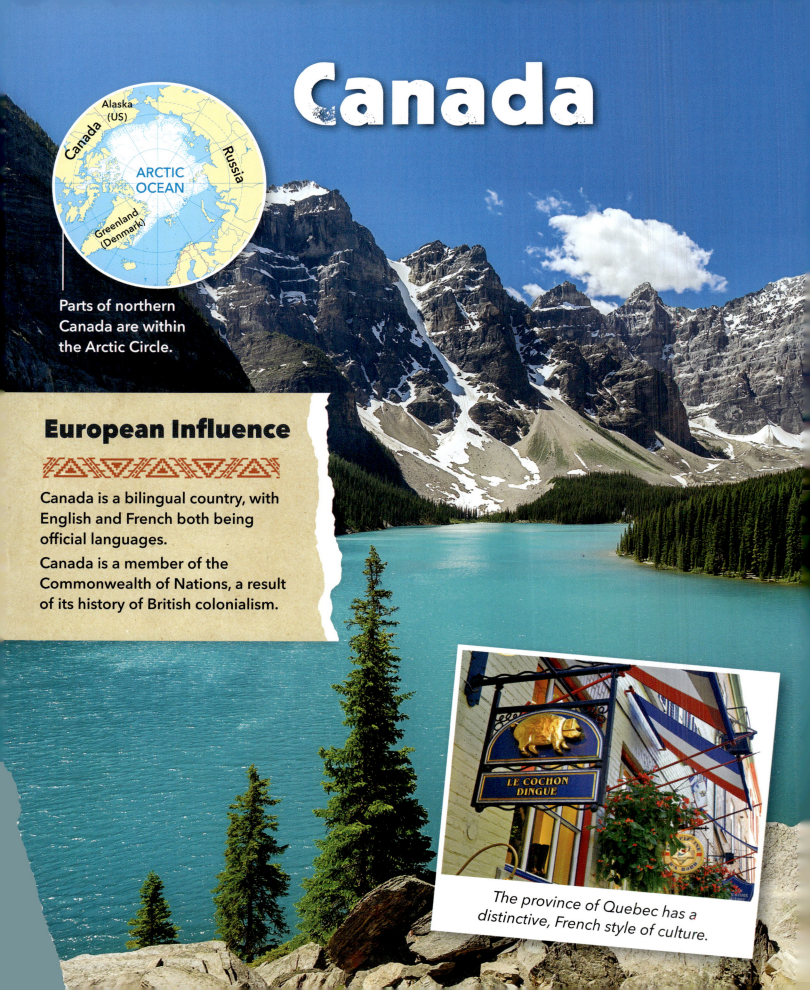

Parts of northern Canada are within the Arctic Circle.

European Influence

Canada is a bilingual country, with English and French both being official languages.

Canada is a member of the Commonwealth of Nations, a result of its history of British colonialism.

The province of Quebec has a distinctive, French style of culture.

Greenland

Greenland is a large country to the north of Canada. It is usually included in the geographical region of North America because it lies on the same tectonic plate.

Inuit Heritage

Greenland's total population is under 60,000, and most Greenlanders have indigenous Inuit heritage.

Greenland is a self-governing territory of Denmark in Europe. This stamp printed in Greenland depicts Queen Margrethe II of Denmark, circa 1973.

A Frozen Landscape

The vast, icy interior of Greenland is uninhabited. The ice sheet covering the country is the second largest on Earth.

Mexico

Climate
The climate ranges from arid desert in the north, where it borders the United States, to tropical in the south.

Language
Mexico has the largest number of Spanish-speaking people in the world.

Ancient Empire
Mexico City was at the centre of the ancient Aztec empire. Spanish conquistadors destroyed much of the Aztec city in the 1500s.

The Pyramid of Kukulcan at the Chichen Itza archaeological site

United States

Democracy
The United States prides itself on being a defender of the democratic style of government. Mount Rushmore in South Dakota (pictured below), is a massive sculpture of four acclaimed presidents who proudly served the democratic process.

State of the Nation

The United States developed from a group of colonies in the 1700s into a country that is very influential in worldwide commerce and culture. It currently has the world's largest economy.

A Land Apart
The state of Hawaii in the Pacific Ocean is part of the United States but not part of the North American continent.

Religions

The Caribbean
The Spanish and French history of much of the Caribbean has resulted in Roman Catholicism being the religion with the largest number of followers in that region.

Alto Vista Roman Catholic Chapel in Aruba

Central America
In Central America, the early Spanish colonisation has resulted in Roman Catholicism being the most popular religion.

Holy Week procession in Guatemala

The USA and Canada
Across the United States and Canada, Christianity is the main religion. In Canada, Roman Catholics have the highest numbers. In the United States, half the whole population follow Protestant Christian religions.

St. Patrick's Roman Catholic Cathedral in New York

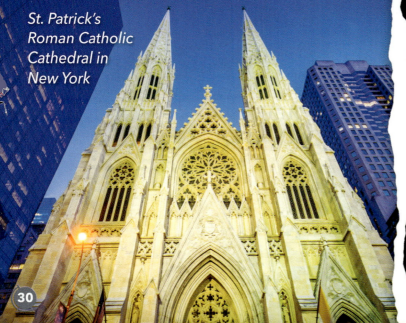

Regional Religions
Local, regional religions are also very popular amongst the Caribbean's people.

A Vodou ceremony

Glossary

arctic climate   very cold climate with large amounts of snow and ice

arid climate   having a very low rainfall

colonise   move into an area and impose a culture on the people already there

democracy   style of government in which the people elect their leaders

geyser   hot water and steam that burst from a spring

gorge   narrow valley with high, rocky sides

nautical mile   term used to measure distance over water or when travelling in the air. It measures 1.85 kilometres

ocean abyss   very deep part of an ocean

plantation   large area where only one type of crop is grown

plate tectonics   movement of large blocks of land across the Earth

temperate climate   mild climate

tropical climate   hot, wet climate

tsunami   huge ocean wave that floods across land

Arctic climates have large amounts of snow

Geysers are hot springs that emit steam and water

Grand Canyon

Index

Appalachian Mountains 15
Aztecs 28
Bering Strait 9
Christopher Columbus 7, 11
climate 6, 19, 28, 31
continental shelf 8, 9, 24
coral reef 24
corn 23
Grand Canyon 18
Great Lakes 19
Greenland 6, 7, 27
indigenous Americans 11, 23, 27

Laurasia 5
Mexico 5, 27, 28
Mount St Helens 17
Niagara Falls 22
Northwest Passage 21
Pacific Ring of Fire 16
Panama Canal 20
plate tectonics 5, 16, 17, 27, 31
population 7, 10, 27, 30
Rocky Mountains 14
San Andreas Fault 16
The Great Plains 23
UNCLOS 8
West Indies 7
Yellowstone National Park ... 17

Niagara Falls